IMAGINATION IN ART

George Taylor

CHERRYTREE BOOKS

A Cherrytree book

Designed and reproduced by Touchstone Publishing Ltd

Copyright this edition © Evans Brothers Ltd 2003
Published by Cherrytree Press Ltd, a division of Evans Brothers
2A Portman Mansions
Chiltern St
London WIU 6NR

First published in 1994
First paperback edition published 2003

Designer: David Armitage
Cover designer: Simon Borrough

Cover picture: *Strelitzia*, David Armitage

British Library Cataloguing in Publication Data
Taylor, George
        Imagination in Art. – (In Art Series)
        I. Title II. Series
        707

        ISBN 1 84234 180 4

Printed in China through Colorcraft Ltd., Hong Kong

Contents

In every chapter of this book you will find a number of coloured panels. Each one has a symbol at the top to tell you what type of panel it is.

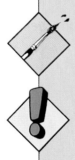

Activity panel Ideas for projects that will give you an insight into the techniques of the artists in this book. Try your hand at painting, sculpting and crafts.

Information panel Detailed explanations of particular aspects of the text, or in-depth information on an artist or work of art.

Look and See panel Suggestions for some close observation, using this book, the library, art galleries, and the art and architecture in your area.

Imagination! It's something we all have, and something we all use all the time. But what is it? In its simplest form, it's what you're doing right now – thinking. Say someone tells you, me and a group of friends a story about being frightened by a big hairy dog. It could be a true story or completely made up. Each person listening will see in their mind an image of a big dog. Take the dog you yourself can 'see'. You don't really 'see' it, you have used

◄ *The ruler of Venice was called the doge, and he was almost as powerful as the pope. Employing a great artist was a way of showing how important you were. During the 16th century, many great Italian artists worked for important people either in Venice or in Rome. Although a portrait painter only painted what he saw, he was often expected to make his sitter appear as heroic or dignified as possible.*
[Doge Leonardo Loredan, *Giovanni Bellini*]

your imagination – the ability to make pictures appear inside your own head. But it's not quite that simple. The chances are that the dog that you imagine is different from the one I imagine, and both yours and mine are quite different from the one imagined by anyone else.

Using your head

This book is about how artists (including painters, sculptors, photographers, computer animators and film-makers) turn their imagination into works of art. Where do their ideas come from? Sometimes an idea will come entirely from the artist's own imagination – from a dream or a nightmare. Sometimes a work of art will be inspired by other people's experiences, or from made-up stories like our one about the frightening dog. Sometimes it may be a mixture of both. And there will be different reasons for creating a work of the imagination. It could be to entertain – to make us feel happy or sad or even frightened. It could be to educate – to show us something we've never seen or thought about before.

Face values

Look at the works of art in this chapter. They all take the human face as their subject. The fact that no two human faces are the same does not explain completely why these works are so different. One reason is that artists use many different tools and materials. Giovanni Bellini, painting hundreds of years ago, had to make his own paint. It was expensive and difficult to use, but it was fine enough to allow him to work in great detail. The modern American painter Willem de Kooning, on the other hand, worked on large canvases with pre-prepared paint that he could apply thickly, straight from the tube if he wanted to.

But if we look more closely, we'll find other reasons why these works of art differ so much. An important question is what were they for? What purpose did they serve? Bellini's painting of the Doge of Venice dates from the days before photography. If you wanted a record of what you looked like, you had your portrait painted. Bellini's painting is as realistic as any photograph, and as long-lasting as many a tombstone – a memorial to the greatness of the man he painted.

▶ *People in Africa have many different religions, and various ceremonies to do with farming their land and rearing their children. By wearing a mask like this one, they might ask for help from their ancestors (the very first members of a tribe) or good luck from a particular god – a god of rain or a fertility god.* [Fang, Congo mask]

He used his eye for colour and detail, but he didn't have to use much imagination. He just had to paint what he saw.

The African mask has a completely different purpose. It is not a portrait of a particular person – the features are not detailed enough for that. But it has been deliberately carved to look part human and part something else. A god, perhaps? Or an ancestor? The mask connects the people who made it to another world. It intentionally mixes up the real, everyday world with an imaginary one. The Yoruba people of Nigeria have a special word for this type of art – *jijora*.

Signs and symbols

Another way to explain the function of the African mask is to say that it is symbolic. A symbol is another word for a sign. There are symbols all around us. If you see a sign for a petrol station or a fast-food restaurant, you will recognize the company name without having to read it.

A cross on the roof of a church is a sign. Even colours can be symbolic. Think of traffic lights: red for 'stop', green for 'go'. The African mask is like a sign. It points you in the direction of a story from the past or from another world and takes you there… but only in your imagination!

▶ *The title tells us that this is a picture of a woman. But would you know that if there were no title? How? Picasso has made no attempt to make the woman's head look three-dimensional. The colours and shapes are flat, so that we are aware that as well as being a painting, this is also a flat rectangle with paint on it. Now look at the painting by Bellini again (page 4). It's almost impossible to see this picture as a flat rectangle, because the painting is so realistic.* [Woman in a Hat, Pablo Picasso]

The Spanish painter Picasso experimented with symbolism. Although many times in his life he changed the way in which he painted, he returned again and again to the same subject – the female figure. The model for the picture on page 7 may well have been his wife at the time. He turned the face into a set of signs – circles for eyes, a rectangle for the head. He used his imagination to do this, but we, too, have to use our imagination. We have to fit the shapes together in our own heads.

Willem de Kooning's paintings often seem to be about the activity of painting itself. Violent colours and strong brushstrokes make you look at the paint on the canvas as much as at the subject depicted. But de Kooning always took reality as the starting point for his painting. Like Picasso and the makers of the African mask, the painter has used his imagination to make us look differently at something we might have taken for granted.

Imagination is a way of passing on ideas and information. A work of art is born in the artist's imagination

▼ If you look at any photograph or film poster of Marilyn Monroe, you will notice her blonde hair and bright red lipstick. What do you notice first about the painting? The blonde hair and bright red lips are there, symbolizing the great star, but looking at this painting is not the same experience as looking at a photograph. Can you describe the difference? [Marilyn Monroe, *Willem de Kooning*]

and made real with paint or with other materials. When we see the result, it becomes part of our imagination. When you look at each of the works of art in this book, ask yourself these questions: What does the artist want to tell me? Why does the artist want to tell me this? How does the artist tell me this?

Experiments with style

Look again at the pictures in this chapter. They are all portraits, but they are all very different. Experiment to see how many different ways, or styles, you can find to paint the same thing. Instead of portraits, try a still-life – several objects grouped together.

What you need
- paint, paintbrushes and water, or pens and pencils
- sketch pad or several sheets of paper
- several objects grouped together on a table. They can be fruit and vegetables, or boxes, tins and packages

What you do
1 First draw or paint what you see as accurately as possible.
2 With your first picture close at hand, begin a second picture, this time simplifying what you see. Work from both the still-life and your first picture.
3 Try again, simplifying even more. Your apples and oranges, boxes and tins could become just circles and squares of colour. Move these shapes around on your paper. Try changing their colours.
4 Paint as many versions of the still-life as you like. Look at the last one. Is it a picture of the original still-life, or is it something different? An interesting pattern? How does it differ from your original picture? In what ways are the two similar?

2 The spirit world

Where did we come from? Why are we here? Where are we going? These questions have puzzled human beings for thousands of years. There are no simple answers. The answers we give depend on our background and beliefs.

What do you believe?

Spiritual belief goes back to the time before scientists knew how to explain natural events such as thunder, lightning, rain and snow. These dramatic phenomena emanating from the sky were a great mystery to our ancestors, sparking off imaginative ideas about their origin. Some unseen supernatural thing or being from another world must surely be directing events in our world. Believing in another world was a way of making sense of this one. For many people, it still is.

This other world could be the home of a god or gods or the place where we go when we die. Some people call it heaven. But it exists only in our imagination, because nobody has ever been there and come back to tell us what it was like. The huge variety of interpretations of the spirit world and its inhabitants has provided artists with endless material for their work.

The world of Greek gods

Some people believe that gods lived in our world before we were here. The stories of their adventures are passed on from one generation to the next. This was true of the ancient Greeks who believed in a whole array of gods. Their myths explain how the gods interfered in the lives of human beings, helping or hindering them at will.

Sculptures and paintings of religious stories were especially important in times when few people could read. Artists painted pictures to tell people religious stories and teach them about their religion. The stained glass windows of a Christian cathedral, for instance, usually tell the life story of Jesus – the story of his birth, the things he

▲ *In the 17th and 18th centuries, stories from ancient Greece and Rome became popular subjects for paintings, especially for murals on the walls and ceilings of stately homes and palaces. The Italian painter Tiepolo was one of the great masters of this kind of painting. This ceiling shows how the goddess Athene gave the young hero Bellerophon a winged horse called Pegasus to help him kill a monster. From our viewpoint, we can imagine that we are looking up and seeing the action taking place on a rocky ledge.*
[Bellerophon slaying the Chimaera, *Giovanni-Battista Tiepolo*]

did during his lifetime, and finally his death on the cross. While people worshipped, they could look at the beautiful windows glowing in the sunlight and reflect on the life of Jesus. Some Christians also believe in hell, where wicked people will face an eternity of torment and terrifying demons. The horrors of hell have been effectively interpreted by many artists including the 15th-century Dutch artist Hieronymus Bosch. There is a painting by Bosch on page 18.

Creation myths

Where people share the same beliefs, it becomes a religion. There are hundreds of different religions all over the world, yet they have in common a surprising number of characters and stories.

Perhaps the oldest religious stories are creation myths that tell how the universe and our world began and how living things came to be. In India, Tara is a 'mother goddess'. She symbolizes the Earth itself, the mother of us all, and she feeds us with the plants she grows. This is a very old idea found in many religions. The ancient Egyptians believed the sun god Ra created the world, but they were equally devoted to the mother goddess Isis. The Greeks also had a mother-goddess, whom they called Gaia. Mary, the mother of Jesus, in the New Testament has a similar role in the Christian religion. In many pictures of her, you will also find flowers, often red and white roses, which symbolize the blood of Christ on the cross and the purity of the Virgin.

When people saw these pictures, they would find many different things to look at (like the roses) which would remind them of other parts of the story. Such things may mean little to us when we study them today, but finding these symbols is part of the fun of looking at works of art and understanding how the painter has used imagination

to present more than the eye can at first see. Many of the pictures in this book contain signs and symbols. The more you learn about the pictures, the more you can see in them.

An angel to watch over me

Many people believe that heaven is above us in the sky. One way of getting there, or getting closer, would be to fly. As a result, certain birds have become religious symbols that appear again and again in

◄ *There are many versions of Tara in both the Hindu and Buddhist religions. She is often represented as a goddess of compassion, as a protector against evil and a mother figure. This 10th-century stone sculpture shows her as a beautiful woman with two children.*

Angels
Winged beings can be seen in the art of many different regions, including China and the Middle East. Books from early Christianity divided angels into nine categories. At the top and nearest to God were the most important, and at the bottom were the protectors and messengers to Earth. Most angels take human form, but Seraphim and Cherubim appear as winged heads only. *Putti* are small naked boys, sometimes winged, who often appear in Christian paintings in minor angelic roles, such as escorting the souls of people up through the clouds to heaven.

paintings. For instance, the eagle is the most worshipped animal among the American Indians. Eagles can be seen on their totem poles. The dove is the symbol for the presence of God in the Christian world, and this too appears in many religious pictures.

Religious stories, and the paintings that depict them, often feature angels. The word angel comes from the Greek word *angelos* – meaning messenger. These winged beings supposedly come and go between our world and heaven, bringing help and good news. It was the angel Gabriel who told Mary that she was pregnant. The archangel Michael was the guardian of the Hebrew people. He is often shown

◄ *St Michael's struggle for good against evil is often described as the battle between the forces of light and darkness. See how the saint's armour and jewels reflect the light. Look for the reflection of buildings and tall spires in his breast-plate. This is the 'holy city' – what we would now call heaven. The dragon represents the devil. The kneeling man is probably the artist's patron, a rich man who would have had the picture painted for his own private chapel or his local church.*
[St Michael and the Dragon, *Bartolomeo Bermejo*]

13

Pre-Raphaelites

Carlos Schwabe, artist of the picture below, painted in a similar style to a group of British artists of the same period (mid-19th century) called the Pre-Raphaelite Brotherhood. Although one of the stated aims of this group was a return to nature, their work often featured imaginary characters acting in scenes from literature, religion or mythology.

The most famous artists were William Holman Hunt, John Everett Millais and Dante Gabriel Rossetti. See if you can find some of their paintings in art books or at a museum. You will see that they always used bright colours and very clear detail. Can you say in what ways these techniques affect the mood of the pictures?

◀ *The artist makes the Angel of Death look both terrifying and spectacular, with huge black wings that appear to clasp her victim. This extraordinary imaginary being is carefully painted with realistic detail. We feel we could reach out and touch her. The green flame is the soul of the dying man, ready for its last journey to eternity. The man's earthly body has only a short trip to make, back into the grave he's been digging. The fact that the angel apparently cannot feel the cold even with her bare feet shows she is untouched by this world.*
[The Angel of Death, *Carlos Schwabe*]

driving the devil, Lucifer, out of heaven. Some people believe that when we die angels come to take our souls to heaven if we deserve it.

Another ancient belief was that the soul of a dying person 'falls in love' with the Angel of Death, and leaves its body willingly.

A spirit mask

Imagine you and your friends have your own mythology, with its own stories, characters and terrifying beasts. You can create your own festivals of dancing and singing, and act out your stories. Enter into the spirit of your festival by making and wearing a mask.

What you need
- piece of card big enough to cover your face
- scissors or a craft knife
- lengths of elastic
- paint, paintbrushes and water
- ribbons, sequins, beads and so on (optional)

What you do

1 Draw an outline of a face on the card. Then draw in features. They could be of an animal god, a devil or an angel. Get the eyes in the right place for you to see through.

2 Decorate the face with paints. Use bright colours to make it as dramatic as possible. Stick on decorative pieces of material or ribbons, if you like.

3 When the paint is dry, cut out the eyes so you can see through. Use plenty of newspaper or a cutting board underneath your mask. Ask for help if you need it, and be careful with the scissors.

4 Cut out the mask. Make little holes on each side (roughly where your ears are) and thread a length of elastic through. Make it long enough to go round your head.

3 Dreams and nightmares

In an average life-span we will spend about 25 years asleep, and out of that nearly six years dreaming! Some nights we may think we haven't had a dream, but in fact we all dream for two or three hours every night. Often our dreams are vivid and easy to recall. They may contain recognizable characters, but these are likely to be involved in strange stories that are set in a place we have never seen before. Many artists turn these weird and wonderful adventures into extraordinary works of art.

Dreaming messages

Why do we dream? Doctors and scientists think that our brains file away all our thoughts from the day, just as a computer tidies up when it is shut down for the night. Or perhaps the brain tries to work out a problem we have been worrying about. When we wake up, we may feel better and know what to do.

Aboriginals and 'dreamtime'

Dreams are very important in Australian Aboriginal culture. Stories about their ancestors and the legendary journeys they made come to Aboriginals while they sleep. But these are not what we think of as dreams. To the Aboriginals, 'the dreaming' is like an ancient map of their land. The landscape itself – every little hill and bump – is part of a story or a journey. The journeys are sometimes called 'songlines', because they are told in songs and poems, as well as paintings.

To those who are unfamiliar with them, dreamtime paintings look like decorative patterns. But they are much more than that. Each dot of colour is important. It may symbolize anything from a footprint, to a person, a bowl of food or an egg. The stories involve god-like ancestors such as the 'Rainbow Serpents', the 'Lightning Men' or the 'Wagilag Sisters'. Bright, unnatural colours are used to suggest the magical powers of these characters. An Aboriginal who sees the painting will instantly recognize the story it tells.

In Europe and America, the way in which artists have painted has changed and developed. But Australian Aboriginal paintings have looked more or less the same for thousands of years. This is because, until the European settlers arrived in Australia 200 years ago, the Aboriginals had no contact with other groups of people. It is only in the last 30 years that Aboriginal art has been seen outside Australia. Even now, their paintings do not get the attention they deserve, because so few people understand them.

▲ *Like many Aboriginal paintings, this work tells the story of a search for food. Seven sisters find a cave (shown in the middle of the painting) with witchetty grubs (edible Australian delicacies) going in and out of it. The seven sisters are shown as V-shapes, each with her own spear. There are three above the cave, three below it and one to the right of it. On the left of the painting are two serpents that the sisters met on their journey to the cave.* [Seven Sisters Dreaming, *Betty Liddle*]

Although this is a modern idea, it has long been thought that we receive messages in our dreams. The Bible tells the stories of many characters who heard God's voice while they were asleep. Jacob, for instance, fell asleep and dreamt of a ladder going up to heaven. Angels were going up and down the ladder, and at the top he saw God who told him that his children would inherit the land.

Jacob's many adventures have been depicted by various artists. One version of Jacob's Ladder was painted by the 19th-century British artist William Blake.

Dreams play a part in many other religions. In South America the god Nai-mu-ena created the world in a dream. In India Brahma, the god of creation, had a similar dream. American Indians tell stories about their gods in songs and poems which, they say, are always the result of a dream.

The Australian Aboriginals have very complicated stories about their people and the lands they live in. They are stories about the journeys their ancestors made and the adventures they had. These come to them when they sleep, in what they call dreamtime (see page 16).

Things that go bump in the night

Sometimes a dream can be so scary that it wakes us up. When we sleep we are helpless and at the mercy of our imagination. This darker side of the human mind revealed in dreams has attracted artists throughout the centuries. Hieronymus Bosch was fascinated by hell and the demons that inhabit it. Some of his paintings are frightening.

St Anthony was a monk who spent his life in solitude. He suffered from terrible visions of demons that attacked him, and from

▲ *Many symbols tell us that this is a picture of St Anthony. He wears the costume of a monk, and a bell (beneath his elbow) to ward off evil spirits. He appears several times in the painting, walking on his own on a path and being taken up into the sky by a strange fish-like creature. People believed he could cure a skin disease which became known as St Anthony's Fire, and this is possibly the reason for the fire in the distance.*
[St Anthony, Hieronymus Bosch]

▼ A woman lies asleep, helpless as her imagination takes flight. The ghastly figure sitting on her is an incubus, an evil spirit who visits sleepers. The dramatic lighting and frightening face of the horse all add to the horror of the scene. [The Nightmare, *Henry Fuseli*]

temptations that shook his religious faith. Bosch used his imagination to depict St Anthony's tormented dream world (page 18). In *The Nightmare* (below) the Swiss artist Henry Fuseli shows the horror that can creep up on us while we sleep.

Surrealism

In the 20th century, a group of artists called the Surrealists became interested in dreams. Surrealism put different, unconnected images together in unnatural combinations, in the way that dreams often do. Artists such as Salvador Dali and Giorgio de Chirico had seen the paintings of Bosch and Fuseli which seemed to them to be inspired by dreams. They also read about the work of an Austrian doctor called Sigmund Freud who had begun to study people's dreams and what they could remember of their early life. This study became known as

Picturing dreams

The writing beneath this picture by Dürer says that, on the night of 7 June 1525, he had such a terrible dream of torrential rain and flooding that he woke up horrifed. The artist often suffered from nightmares. The picture has the feeling of having been sketched very quickly before Dürer had time to forget his dream.

Why don't you try to remember a dream or nightmare and turn it into a drawing or painting? It might help to keep a sketchbook by your bed so that you can sketch your dream the minute you wake up.

psychoanalysis. Freud wanted to find a link between the normal behaviour of his patients and what was happening in their subconscious – the thoughts going on in their heads that they were not aware of. Under hypnosis, Freud's patients revealed the contents of their imagination to him: their memories of childhood, their hopes, fears and loves, their dreams and nightmares.

For the Surrealists, this opened up a whole new world to paint. De Chirico wrote that 'if a work of art is to be truly immortal, it must pass quite beyond the limits of the human world, without any common sense or logic. In this way the work will draw nearer to the dream'.

▼ *It is often impossible to say what a Surrealist painting means. Often the very title is chosen to mislead us. Perhaps Dali is trying to suggest the floating feeling we sometimes have when we are asleep. But don't forget that the artist also enjoyed a good joke! Can you see any connections between this picture and Bosch's painting on page 18?*
[Sleep, *Salvador Dali*]

Many people disliked the work of the Surrealists. They thought that they painted whatever they wanted, without feeling the need to explain themselves. Perhaps that was the point the Surrealists were making. A dream is personal. Surrealism encouraged people to feel free to explore their own dreams and nightmares.

Freud tried to help his patients in a similar way. He and his followers believed that understanding our dreams is a step towards a better understanding of ourselves.

Surrealist painters
Surrealist paintings are about the interpretation of dreams. Find pictures by other Surrealist artists, such as Giorgio de Chirico, René Magritte and John Armstrong, and compare them with the Dali picture here and others you may come across. (There is one in the book *Places in Art* in this series.)

Are there any similarities between them, in style or in content? Or does it seem that dreams are so personal that each painting is completely individual?

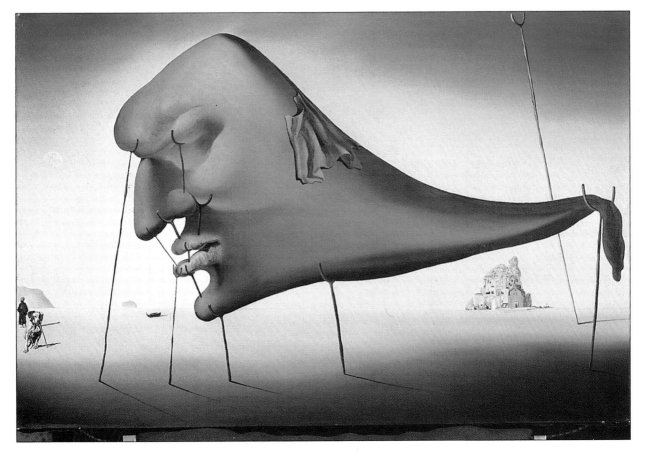

4 Believe it or not?

All art is deception. A sculptor tries to make a block of marble not look like a block of marble. A painter tries to make a flat, square canvas not look like a flat, square canvas. We often take this deception for granted. The more skilfully the trick is played on us, the less we notice it. Look again at Bellini's painting on page 4. Bellini used all his technical skills to make the portrait look as realistic and as lifelike as possible so that we would forget it was a flat picture.

A trick of the eye

When a picture is obviously intended to deceive us we call it a *trompe l'oeil* – a trick played on the eye. A *trompe l'oeil* painting could be anything from fake classical columns painted on a wall to a huge, imaginary landscape. The artist tries to create what's called 'pictorial space'. This is a way of making a flat picture appear very deep, so that what's in the painting appears to be a long way behind the picture frame. It is almost as if we were looking through a

Perspective

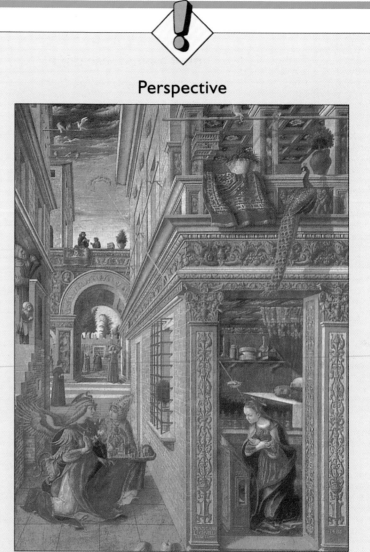

To see how perspective works, take a ruler and place it so that it crosses the feet of the tiny figure dressed in a brown cloak in the distance. Which ever way you rotate your ruler around that point, you will find that it will be in line with the edges of all the buildings. This point is called the 'vanishing point'.

Look at some buildings and work out where your own vanishing point is. It will be directly in front of you at eye-level. Perspective was an important discovery for architects, because it meant they could draw how a building would look to the eye, before it was built.
[Annunciation, *Carlo Crivelli*]

▼ *Here we are standing on a terrace, overlooking a beautiful garden. Or are we? Look again. The pair of doors in the middle of the picture is a clue. In fact, this is an elaborate* trompe l'oeil. *Everything behind the chairs and the marble statue is painted on a curved wall. Even the classical pillars are fake. This decorative technique was popular in grand houses in the 18th century.* [Round dining room in the garden pavilion of the Comptess de Provence at Montreuil, Versailles]

window at another world beyond. Often a *trompe l'oeil* is painted on the wall of a room to make it look much bigger than it really is. So a room in a small town house might contain a *trompe l'oeil* of a window opening on to a beautiful garden. A real window in the same room would only open out on to more houses.

A new perspective

Five hundred years ago European artists found new ways of making their paintings and sculptures more realistic. This period of history, called the Renaissance (meaning 'rebirth'), was a time when artists rediscovered the art of ancient Rome and Greece, and marvelled at how lifelike it was. An Italian architect, Brunelleschi, devised 'perspective', a mathematical method of calculating pictorial space. In the western world it changed painting and the way people looked at the world for ever. We know that objects that are near look bigger than objects further away.

Perspective allowed artists to place these objects in a pictorial space that made sense to our eyes.

Tricks and games

Since the invention of perspective, we've become used to seeing the real world reproduced realistically in pictures. In modern times, artists have found other ways to deceive us, using tricks of the imagination. Our imagination, of course, deceives us all the time. In the last chapter we discussed how the Surrealists mixed up the real and imaginary in their paintings. Their paintings disturb us because they are not what we expect.

The Dutch artist M C Escher was also inspired by the idea of deceiving the eye. The buildings in his pictures look realistic. But a closer look reveals that they would be impossible to build. However long you look at one of his structures, you will never solve the puzzle.

Fakes and forgeries

Not all deceptions are meant to be amusing. Almost as soon as photography was invented, people began to forge

photographs. This was trickery on a grand scale. Everybody believes that what they see in a photograph is real. In one famous case in the 1920s two girls, Elsie Wright and Frances Griffiths, reported that they had seen fairies at the bottom of their garden. Nobody believed them – until they saw the photographs that seemed to prove it. Among those who were convinced by this hoax was the famous author of the

▲ *Look carefully at the waterfall. The water falls into a mill pond, flows along a channel, round several corners and then... turns into the waterfall. Such a building could never exist in reality.* [Waterfall, *M C Escher*]

Sherlock Holmes detective stories, Sir Arthur Conan Doyle. For many years afterwards people argued about whether the photographs were genuine, but it was not until the 1980s that it was proved beyond doubt that the photographs had been cleverly faked when the two girls – by then quite elderly – owned up!

Over the years, the photographs have often been reproduced, even though they were acknowledged fakes. But newspaper editors know that people are always interested in seeing pictures of creatures they thought existed only in the imaginary world.

The picture on the page

What do you remember about your favourite children's stories? A story or a novel is a work of fiction. It is not true, and yet the author writes so powerfully that we enter into the world of the book, willingly letting ourselves be deceived, wanting to turn the pages and find out what happens in this imaginary world. When the book is illustrated the artist helps the author deceive the reader. After we have read the book, we always imagine the characters as they looked in the pictures. A young child today might imagine the characters in fairy tales like Snow White and the Seven Dwarfs or Aladdin as they appeared in the cartoon film versions, rather than the original stories.

The American artist N C Wyeth was a very successful illustrator. He enjoyed depicting

▼ *This photograph is a fake. Using earlier paintings of imagined fairies as their inspiration, the two young photographers made a little cardboard cut-out model which was placed in front of one of the girls. It was held in place with a hat-pin!*

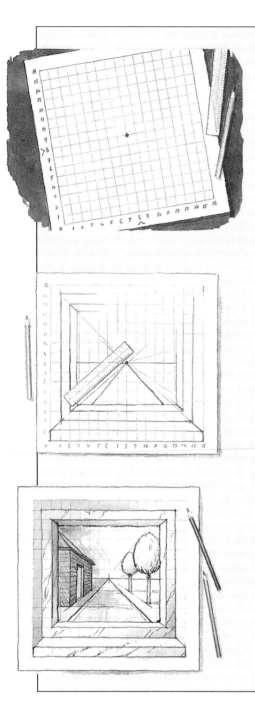

Trompe l'oeil using perspective

Imagine you are going to paint a *trompe l'oeil* picture on a wall. First you must design it by sketching it on a grid. Then, by drawing a larger grid on the wall, your design can be redrawn on a larger scale. Copy our landscape to start with, then try your own *trompe l'oeil* picture.

What you need
- piece of paper (you can use graph paper)
- pencil
- ruler

What you do
1 Draw a grid of squares that fits your paper. Try 16cm x 16cm divided into 1cm squares. Numbering each line from 1 to 16 may help you.
2 Find the centre point, where the two 8cm lines cross over. This is your vanishing point.
3 If you like you can draw an attractive frame for the grid. It could be like an old picture frame or like the classical pillars in the painting on page 23. Using the centre point and your ruler, draw lines to each corner of your frame. This gives your frame a 'thickness'.
4 In the middle of the frame, draw a landscape or a beautiful garden. Using what you have learnt about perspective, you could try drawing a building. Place it off-centre, to one side or the other. You can use the grid lines to draw the side of the building nearest you. Using your ruler and the vanishing point, draw in the other wall.
5 If you were painting a mural, you would now draw your grid on the wall and copy your picture on to it, square by square. Remember, you would have to scale it up. Each 1cm square would become 10cm. And you would need a longer ruler!

imaginary characters and exciting events from adventure stories. Some of his most famous illustrations were drawn for Robert Louis Stevenson's *Treasure Island*. There are plenty of clues in the story as to what the characters looked like physically, but Wyeth had to use his own imagination to turn them into believable characters, dress them and create backgrounds for them.

Stories to illustrate

Could you illustrate a story? Get someone to read you a story from a picture book, one you don't know, and illustrate some scenes from it. Imagine the characters and the world they live in. Think carefully about the detail. Now look at the printed illustrations in the book. Are your ideas anything like those of the original artist? How are they the same? How do they differ? Do you prefer seeing the results of someone else's imagination, or imagining your own characters?

▶ *The pirate Long John Silver leads cabin boy Jim Hawkins off to captivity. Stevenson describes the character of Long John Silver in his story, but the artist had to decide what he would wear. The scene is full of action and movement, something words alone cannot provide. The strong contrast of sunlight and shadow makes the illustration look three-dimensional so that it stands out against the black and white text on the 'flat' page next to it.* [The Hostage. *'For all the world, I was led like a dancing bear'.* Illustration by N C Wyeth from Treasure Island, *by Robert Louis Stevenson*]

5 Better than nature?

We have all stood looking at a landscape and said 'if only that ugly building weren't there', or 'the countryside is beautiful, but I wish it weren't raining!' Artists often think the same thoughts when they paint a landscape, only they can do something about it!

The period from 1750 to 1850 was a time of great change in the world. There were revolutions and uprisings. In France, poor people took up arms and fought their king. And there was a revolution of another kind – the Industrial Revolution. Factories belched out smoke and fire, lighting up the sky at night. Men, women and even children worked long hours in terrible conditions.

▲ *If you look carefully at this painting, you can see some people far off in the distance. They are so small, you hardly notice them. So why have them at all? Perhaps it helps to show how big the landscape is, and how tiny and unimportant we are compared to nature.*
[Imaginary Landscape, *Thomas Doughty*]

28

The artist's changing world

At the same time, the place of the artist in this world was changing. There had always been two classes of people, the rich and the poor. Artists and craftspeople usually came from the poorer class. Although they might become quite rich from their skills, they were at the mercy of kings, popes and other rich people who employed them. The French Revolution helped to create a new class of people called the middle class, or *bourgeoisie.* They were skilled people: politicians, philosophers, doctors, lawyers – and artists. Some artists became wealthy and had time to paint what they wanted to paint as well as what someone else paid them to paint.

Romantic landscapes

Landscape gave the painter a greater artistic freedom than portrait paintings or religious paintings which had to follow strict rules and please a patron. With landscape, the artist could question whether the new industrial society was better than the old rural way of life. To make their point, the artists had to use their imagination.

Some landscape paintings are called 'romantic', because they show scenery which is wild, or desolate, or filled with some kind of deep feeling. These paintings bore little

The Serpent Mound

The Ohio earthwork is between 2000 and 3000 years old. Nobody knows what the mound was for. It must have been very important because of the amount of time and hard work that was needed to build it. In Native American religions, the snake symbolizes the power to live for ever. The people believed that snakes had this ability because they felt that the way they shed their skins so many times symbolized a constant renewal of life.

relation to reality. The American painter Thomas Doughty probably began a picture like the one on page 28 by making sketches from real life. He would draw a stream he liked, a tree, then a mountain, and then combine the separate drawings to make one picture. He would exaggerate everything, making the mountainsides steeper and more dramatic than they really were. He would make the trees bushier than in nature. He even added the old, ruined castles he had seen on his travels in Europe, even though there weren't any in America. They were symbols of the old world which he felt was being lost.

The Ancients

Samuel Palmer was a member of a small group of romantic painters called the Ancients. Like Doughty, he believed that industrialization was separating people from their feeling for nature. The Ancients talked of painting feelings. Like the Aboriginals, Samuel Palmer saw himself as

▼ *Light is very important in this picture. It is twilight, the most romantic time of the day, when the light is fading and the workers are coming home from the fields. Even so, their farm is still lit up, with a warm, friendly glow. The people in the picture, and even the oxen's horns, are all pointing towards the farm, and we feel as if we are following on behind.* [The Bellman with Oxen, *Samuel Palmer*]

A stylized landscape

In this chapter we have seen how some romantic artists made their landscapes look more dramatic than they were in reality. You can play around with reality too. Make a scene look more attractive, or uglier, than it really is. Your school might be a good place to start.

What you need

- sketchbook
- pencil
- watercolours or some other paints
- paintbrush
- watercolour paper

What you do

1 Find an interesting view. It could be a landscape, or a town with buildings. How about a view of your school?
2 Make a detailed sketch of what's in front of you, and then take your drawing back inside.
3 Using your watercolour paper, try making your scene look more attractive. Remove anything you don't like. It could be a telegraph pole or a busy road. Make the colours bright and cheerful. You could make the sky bright blue and the grass greener.
4 Start again on a fresh piece of paper. Now make your scene look worse than it actually is. Put a wash of grey watercolour over the whole picture. To do this, load a thick brush with lots of water and only a dash of grey paint. Apply this quickly in wide brushstrokes across the paper. You could add some factory chimneys and smoke, or some litter, but let the grey wash dry first.

a part of the natural world. His landscape pictures are not paintings of a particular view. They are very stylized. This means that Palmer had a very personal way of painting. He often used black ink, which made the outlines and textures of trees and fields very bold. He used just a few strong colours, which he painted on to the whole canvas, to give the feeling of coloured light falling on the scene. Sometimes it is the clear blue light of the moon; sometimes it is the warm yellow light of the setting sun.

Innocent art

In the 20th century, naïve artists also painted landscapes in a stylized way. Their style of painting was called 'naïve' because it appeared simple and innocent. They didn't bother with perspective or those technical skills that made a painting look realistic. These landscapes start in the imagination of the artist rather than in the real world.

The most famous naïve painter was a French artist called Henri Rousseau. (You can see some of his pictures in *Places in Art* and *Conflict in Art*.) Rousseau painted some

very large pictures of tropical forests, full of huge, leafy plants and wild animals. He told people he had visited Mexico while on army service, but this wasn't true. He got all his inspiration for his paintings from illustrated magazines and from his local botanical garden!

Green fingers

Some artists turn the landscape itself into a work of art. The work of the American Robert Smithson is called Earth art. Like much modern art, the imaginative idea is as important as the actual portrayal of it.

The idea of sculpting the land is very old. There are ancient earthworks all over the world, as well as stone circles such as Stonehenge in Britain. These places are believed to have played a part in religious ceremonies and festivals. Modern Earth art does not have a religious purpose. But it does pose questions for us to answer. Is an ancient stone circle art? What about a bush that has been trimmed into the shape of a bird – is that art? Can a beautifully laid-out garden or park be considered art? Is the *Spiral Jetty* (see opposite page) art? Many

▲ *This is one of four paintings that celebrate the seasons. The artist covers the land with trees and fields of flowers to make us think about the richness and fertility of the soil. Remember how people talk about 'mother nature'? Look again at this picture. Can you see what's hidden in the shape of the hills and valleys? [Spring, Tamás Galambos]*

32

Changing townscapes

Visit your local public library and see if you can find old photos of a town you know. Can you recognize the different views? Towns change constantly. Old buildings are knocked down and new ones are built. Do you think these changes have made the town look better. How? Draw a picture of how you would like your town to look. Throw out any buildings you don't like, and put new ones in.

▶ *What do you think of this work of art? Do you think it would look more interesting if you actually went there, instead of looking at a photograph of it taken from the air? Some people say that there is a dangerous whirlpool in the middle of the lake. Do you think it is important to know this when you look at the picture?*
[Spiral Jetty, *Robert Smithson*]

people don't like modern Earth art. Maybe it's because they don't like being asked questions!

Earth art doesn't usually last very long, because the weather erodes it. All we are left with is a photograph. Sometimes not even that. If you go to the theatre and see the performance of a play, it will last for a few hours and then finish. We can think about Earth art in the same way as a play. The idea in the artist's head is the work of art. When it is turned into a real thing made of mud and stones, it will last a few years and then it will be gone. That was the performance. Art that provides a temporary visual record of an artist's idea is called Conceptual art.

# 6 A modern vision

Before the invention of photography most western artists concerned themselves with painting what they saw as accurately as possible. But photography was even more accurate. Would it signal the end of painting? Not at all. In fact photography gave painting a new lease of life. Artists started to think about their paintings in an entirely different way.

Pictures that move

The Impressionists were a group of painters who studied photography. They liked the way a photograph could capture the feeling of a particular moment. But early black and white photography could not get across the real atmosphere of a landscape. The early Impressionists (notably Monet, Pisarro and Renoir) wanted to give us an

'impression' of how something or someone makes us feel. They wanted to make us see what happens when the sun goes down or light glints on water.

Impressionist paintings sometimes look rushed. The bold brushstrokes may make us think they were painted carelessly, especially when we compare them with a Renaissance painting such as Crivelli's *Annunciation* (see page 22). But the techniques used in these pictures were highly original and required great skill. To capture a moment, the artist had to work fast and confidently. Instead of outlining objects in black as artists always had done in drawings, they now created forms using light and dark paint, with very little outlining. They recorded light falling on objects and the shadows they create.

The end of the 19th century, when Impressionism started, was a time of great change. People travelled more. African and oriental art was being seen in Paris for the first time. Scientists and psychologists were experimenting with colour and seeing how it affects us.

And photography had led to the birth of film.

Art in words
'The first colours that made a strong impression on me were bright, juicy green, white, carmine red, black and yellow ochre. These memories go back to the third year of my life. I saw these colours on various objects which are no longer as clear in my mind as the colours themselves'.

Kandinsky was just one of many modern artists who have written about art. Although he was self-taught, Vincent Van Gogh read an enormous number of books on art and colour theory, and wrote down his own views in a daily diary which he kept for eight years. One of the earliest artists to write about his art was the Italian Benvenuto Cellini. He wrote a boastful autobiography in which he pointed out that he was the most talented artist of his time! Today many modern artists write about their work or are interviewed in newspapers. It can be useful to read or listen to what an artist has to say about his or her own work. Look in your library for books on artists such as Van Gogh, Mondrian, Mark Rothko and David Hockney, and see what comments they make about their paintings. Do these help you understand the pictures?

◄ *There is a great feeling of movement in this Impressionist picture. The direction of the brushstrokes in the clouds and across the trees and bushes suggests a strong wind rushing down the valley. The blurred effect this creates is a bit like the glimpses of the countryside you see out of the window of a fast-moving train or car. Can you imagine what it would feel like to be walking in this landscape?*
[The Gust of Wind, *Pierre Auguste Renoir*]

The Impressionist painters, and the artists who came after them, such as Van Gogh, Gauguin and Seurat, saw painting as another way of experimenting. Renoir worked at capturing movement. Van Gogh and Seurat experimented with colour. Paul Gauguin took ideas from African and Japanese art. All of them worked outdoors to try and capture the effects of sunlight and shade.

Pattern and decoration

Along with the African masks and the oriental prints came patterned textiles from all over the world. For many people, pattern is an important art form. To us, the pattern on a bed cover or on the wallpaper might be just decorative. But to the Aboriginals (see page 17), for example, colourful patterns of dots and shapes hold meaning. The decoration on an African tribesman's shield will show which tribe he's from and how important he is. Often such patterns are symmetrical – if you draw a line down the middle of a design, each half will look the same. Nature is full of symmetry – look at your own face in the mirror for instance!

Gaudier-Brzeska's sculpture is balanced rather than symmetrical, and there is a pattern to it. The eye of the fish and the eye of the bird are the same shape, the two tails point in opposite directions and the shape of the bird's beak is shared with the head of the fish.

▼ *At the beginning of World War I, the sculptor Gaudier-Brzeska was a pacifist – he didn't believe in fighting, whatever the cause was. Later he changed his mind and was sadly killed just a few weeks after signing up to fight. He has made his fish look like a bomb, an image of danger and destruction. Did he imagine that the young men going off to war were willingly swallowing death?* [Bird Swallowing Fish, *Henri Gaudier-Brzeska*]

36

▶ *Mondrian was one of a group of artists that included painters, architects and furniture makers. Although this is an abstract painting, it has the solid simplicity of a modern building. Mondrian was also interested in stained glass. Can you see how this might have affected his work? How does the painting make you feel? Can you imagine what the painter was feeling as he painted the picture?*
[Composition in Red, Blue and Yellow, *Piet Mondrian*]

The Dutch artist Piet Mondrian was also interested in geometric patterns. Many of his paintings are very simple – sometimes just two or three black lines crossing over each other. But this simplicity is very deceptive. The longer you look at the picture, the more you see. Mondrian called this 'pure painting'. Like a pattern, the picture doesn't try to show you anything else (like a landscape), it just shows you itself – a flat square with more flat squares inside it. There is no perspective, and yet you find yourself trying to imagine which square is nearer to you and which is farther away! When there is nothing realistic left in a picture, it is called 'abstract'.

Abstract art

Many painters today have become less interested in painting realistic pictures and more interested in abstraction. Like much of the imaginative art we have already looked at, abstract art often has a starting point in reality. It takes colours and shapes that we find in the

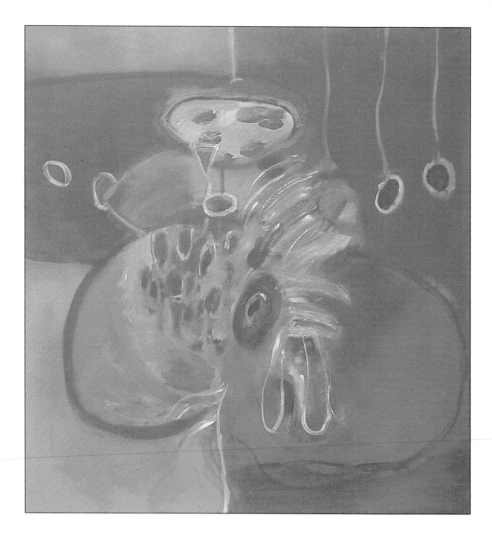

◄ *Although this is an abstract painting, there are shapes in it that might remind you of something you have seen – something real. A strelitzia is a flower (also known as Bird of Paradise) but the artist has used colour and shape in an imaginative way to make the picture look mysterious. This is a recent painting by a living artist, working after de Kooning had painted many of his pictures, after the Surrealists, after Renoir and the Impressionists. Do you think this artist has been inspired by any of them? If so, how?*
[Strelitzia, David Armitage]

real world around us, and puts them together in new patterns.

Painting only what we see is like taking a photograph. It is a souvenir of a place we know, or an accurate record of what someone looked like. Abstract art lets us enter the invisible world of the mind. A world of thoughts and ideas, of feelings and emotions. A world of the imagination. Like the world of dreams the Surrealists tried to paint, it is a world without rules, where anything can happen. And each of us will see something completely different in an abstract painting.

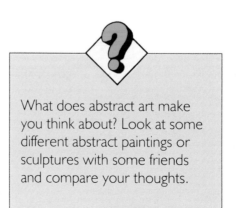

What does abstract art make you think about? Look at some different abstract paintings or sculptures with some friends and compare your thoughts.

Music in paint

Many of Kandinsky's paintings have musical sounding titles, because he considered music to be another type of abstract art. Test this theory by painting abstract pictures to music. You might like to do this activity with some friends and compare the results.

What you need

• collection of different types of music. Choose from rap, rock, a sad ballad, soaring classical music, something angry by a modern composer such as Stockhausen – whatever you like. Get someone to help find the music or tape it from the radio.

• paper   • paint, paintbrushes and water

What you do

1 Put on your first piece of music. Listen to it, decide what colours you need and how it makes you feel.

2 As the music plays, let your brush dance across the paper. Try and express the mood of the piece of music. The rock music may make your brush jerk up and down in rhythm; the classical music may inspire large, sweeping brushstrokes.

3 Do the same for the other pieces of music.

4 You could use your sketches to produce larger paintings expressing the same moods.

[Improvisation No. 19A, *Wassily Kandinsky*]

How do you imagine the world will look in the future? What will happen to art and artists in a world dominated by computer graphics?

When each new invention comes along, whether it's photography, film, animated cartoons or computer games, someone always says it will kill off the art forms that have come before. It never does. People always want pictures around them, whether it's a print of a favourite painting on the bedroom wall, or works of art at an art gallery or museum.

New inventions have always been of interest to artists themselves. Remember how photography inspired the Impressionists? And how perspective excited the Renaissance painters? Today, it is computers that offer a whole new world for the artist's imagination to explore.

Imagining the future

When people use their imagination to create images of the future, the result is called science fiction. There are science fiction books and comics, films and television series. No one knows what the future holds, so the artist has great freedom. It's like painting pictures of heaven or hell – no one knows what they look like either! Trying to predict the future is something human beings have done for thousands of years. You probably know someone who reads their horoscope in the newspaper every day.

Unlike N C Wyeth's illustration for *Treasure Island* on page 27, which included ready-made characters, the science fiction cartoonist can make up new characters. Often the cartoonist will look around at the present world for clues as to what the future might bring. What if the world becomes even more violent? What sort of police force will be needed to deal with crime?

Judge Dredd is an imaginary character, but he is made more powerful by the possibility that, one day, this type of law-enforcer might actually exist.

Future fantasy
Science fiction stories are all around us, especially in comics and on the television. Look at a few with some friends. Are these made-up worlds how you and they imagine the future will be? In reality perhaps the future won't be so different from today. What do you think might be different, what might be the same? Do you think human beings will always look the same?

▶ *Judge Dredd is an imaginary futuristic law-enforcement officer. The idea that the future will be chaotic and out of control, ruled by machines and technology, has become almost traditional. Do you think this fearsome image of Judge Dredd helps us to think about the fate of the world before it is too late?* [Judge Dredd, *from the comic* 2001]

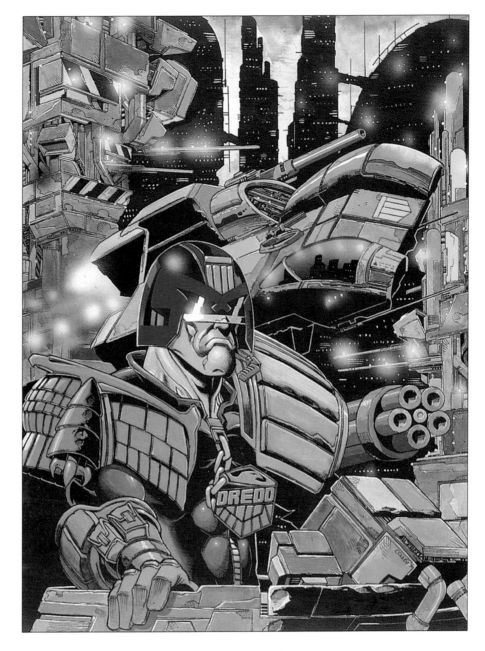

Worlds apart

Before human beings first set foot on the moon in the 1960s, people had strange ideas about how it might look. Some people jokingly said it was made of green cheese! We have now seen pictures of the surface of the moon, so we know what it looks like. But the stars and planets we see at night are millions of light years away, too far for human beings to reach. All we see of them with the naked eye are tiny dots of light. What do these heavenly bodies really look like?

Computer-aided art

The Hubble space telescope on board a satellite can now send back photographs of distant planets and stars. The space agency NASA also receives photographs from the probes it launches into space. But these photographs are only small sections of electronic data that have to be pieced together like a jigsaw puzzle and enhanced by computer to counteract blurring.

With this limited information, artists take over from scientists and create their own impressions of the planets. Using computers, they can work on the photographs, and add their own details of what these worlds might look like.

Although these artists use the latest technology, they work in the same way as Thomas Doughty (page 28) – they make their space landscapes look more interesting than they might be in reality.

▼ *Using photographs and other data from the surface of Saturn, this artist has drawn an impression of how NASA scientists think the planet probably looks. No one knows what the strange rings around the planet look like close to. It is thought they are made up of dust and small rocks floating around in space. It was left to the artist's imagination to portray this in the way he or she thought best. [Artist's concept of Saturn as seen from the ring of Saturn]*

▲ *There are elements that we can recognize in this frame from a computer game – the classical pillared building, the trees, rocks and sea. And yet there is a mysterious feeling of calm. How has the artist achieved this? How do you know there is no wind? Have you ever been on a seashore when it has been this calm? [View of the observatory and boat dock, from the computer game MYST]*

Worlds of fantasy

Using the same technology to create fantasy computer games, artists conjure up worlds that don't exist at all. By putting different photographs into the computer – of trees, hills and lakes – they can create places and situations that look realistic and unusual at the same time. Like a cartoon, they can move. But unlike a cartoon, we can enter this fantasy world and make decisions about where to go and how to direct the game. Computer technology is developing extremely quickly. Each week new games are launched.

The only limit on this art form is the imagination of the artists – and the imagination of the players who enter their strange worlds.

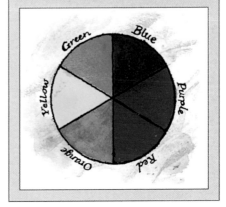
Forwards to the past

Although there are many futuristic computer games, there are many – like *MYST* – that look more like an old forgotten world. When the film *Jurassic Park* was made, people were amazed at the

43

special effects. Real-life dinosaurs chasing people! Well, not really. The film makers used many different types of special effects. There were life-size models that moved mechanically, and others – just as life-like – that existed only inside a computer. Actors had to act scenes, imagining that they were being chased by the dinosaurs. On the screen it looks realistic, but in fact the film clips of the live action and the computer-designed dinosaurs were put together in the editing room.

It took a great deal of time and money to achieve these effects. Film is simply lots of single frames (like photographs) shown one after another so fast that what you see is a moving picture. Each frame in *Jurassic Park* had to be made individually, and shadows drawn in to make the dinosaurs look completely realistic. The designers had real dinosaur skeletons to look at, but they had to decide what their skins looked like, and what colour they were.

▼ *Do you recall how difficult it was to remember that Bellini's picture was painted on a flat canvas, because the three-dimensional portrait was so life-like? In the same way, we're now so used to seeing convincing computer special effects that it is impossible to separate the two images that make up the frame: the actor in a landscape and the computer-animated dinosaurs chasing him. The images merge in our minds because the scene is so realistic.*
[*Still from* Jurassic Park]

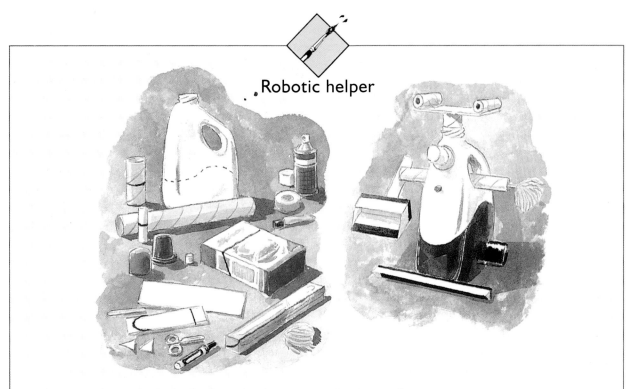

Robotic helper

Robots are not science fiction. They are everywhere. They build our cars, they explore the sea bed, they've even been to the moon. Imagine having your own domestic robot to help you around the house. What would you like it to do? What would it look like?

What you need
- household rubbish - empty boxes and cartons, plastic bottles and containers
- scissors
- glue
- paint – a can of silver spray paint, if possible

What you do

1 It's easy! Just put different parts together to make your robot, but think about it first. What job is it designed for? Imagine it at work. Does it need legs, or wheels or neither? Does it have a head? Is it square, sharp and shiny, or smooth and simple like a modern vacuum cleaner. Play around with different shapes before you glue anything.

2 When you've assembled your robot, glue it together and paint it. If you've worked with light bulbs, batteries and switches before, you might even be able to give your robot a flashing light. (Never use mains electricity – it is dangerous.)

Art is for always

Some people say that if the great Italian painter and inventor Leonardo da Vinci were alive today, he'd be sitting in front of a computer screen. Perhaps he would. But there will always be painters and sculptors – and there will always be computer artists, even when technology moves on again.

A computer is like the artist's palette, a blank canvas, a block of marble and a chisel rolled into one. There are so many different ways to create a work of art. There's only one thing you must have: imagination!

About the artists

ARMITAGE, David (b.1943) Born in Tasmania, David Armitage lived and worked in New Zealand before settling in the UK in 1973. His work is abstract but much of it contains recognizable objects and living things transformed into shapes that are fluid and startling.

BELLINI, Giovanni (c.1430-1516) Although his brother Gentile was known as a portrait painter, and was even made official portrait painter to the doges, Giovanni was the more famous, and was one of only a few Venetian artists interested in the Renaissance revolution of pictorial space and light.

BERMEJO, Bartolomeo (1474-1498) A Spanish artist known for the richness of detail in his work, the characterization of his portraits and their dramatic force.

BOSCH, Hieronymus (c.1450-1516) An extremely distinctive Dutch painter, obsessed with the spiritual extremes of earthly pleasure, temptation, horror and damnation.

CRIVELLI, Carlo (1430/35-1493/1500) An early Renaissance painter, born in Venice, who retained the decorativeness of the previous Gothic style and combined it with the new fascination for creating pictorial space.

DALI, Salvador (1904-1989) Born in Spain, Dali was both a creative genius and outrageous showman, gaining great publicity for the Surrealist movement he joined.

DE KOONING, Willem (b.1904) Born in Holland, de Kooning emigrated to the United States when he was 22, and worked as a commercial artist. His work has always been influenced by a combination of European abstract painting and his interest in the human form.

DOUGHTY, Thomas (1793-1856) One of the earliest American landscape artists to gain an international reputation, and a founder of the Hudson River School.

DÜRER, Albrecht (1471-1528) One of the most important painters in the history of art and, with his editions of woodcuts and engravings of religious stories, the first true commercial artist. Born in Germany, he is also known for his self-portraits and watercolour sketches of landscape.

ESCHER, M C (1898-1972) Escher studied architecture and decorative arts in Holland. He spent much time in Italy, his work mainly occupied with nature. When he returned to Holland in 1937 his work became more surrealist, other-worldly and often gloomy.

FUSELI, Henry (1741-1825) A Swiss painter who spent much of his life in London. Although he was a talented portrait painter, paintings like *The Nightmare*, and his interest in dreams and the fantastic, have caused him to be labelled the forefather of the Surrealists.

GALAMBOS, Tamás (b.1939) A living artist, working in Hungary. His work is more than just naïve art: there are symbolic and political messages in his paintings common to many Eastern European artists of this century.

GAUDIER-BRZESKA , Henri (1891-1915) Tragically killed at 24, the French sculptor Gaudier-Brzeska was a pioneer of abstract sculpture, and was an acknowledged inspiration for another great 20th-century sculptor, Henry Moore. Brzeska was the name of the Polish woman he lived with.

KANDINSKY, Wassily (1866-1944) Kandinsky trained as a lawyer in Russia before travelling extensively and finally settling in France. It was landscape painting that most inspired the young artist, before he became a central figure in abstract painting.

LIDDLE, Betty A living Australian Aboriginal artist who began painting in 1987 after visiting the art galleries of Alice Springs. She now exhibits all over the world – the tribal stories that inspire her paintings were handed down by her grandparents.

MONDRIAN , Piet (1872-1944) A Dutch pioneer of abstraction along with Kandinsky and the Russian artist Malevich. His influence on other artists has been as much from his writings as from his famous geometric paintings of black lines dividing flat planes of white and primary colours.

PALMER, Samuel (1805-1881) An English painter whose interest in nature and rural subjects led him to found a group of artists – 'the Ancients' – which included the artist and writer William Blake.

PICASSO, Pablo (1881-1973) A Spanish artist whose long career and vast output of work has overshadowed the 20th century. His paintings constantly fluctuated between abstraction and realism, and between his interests in classical art and this century's modernism.

RENOIR, Pierre Auguste (1841-1919) A founder member of the French Impressionist movement. Renoir's large output of paintings created a market for his work much earlier than his contemporaries and, consequently, his work is found in collections all over the world.

SCHWABE, Carlos (1866-1926) German born, Schwabe studied in Switzerland, then worked as a successful interior designer in Paris. As well as painting, he also worked as a book illustrator, contributing drawings to editions of *La Rêve* by Zola, and *Les Fleurs du Mal* by Baudelaire.

SMITHSON, Robert (1938-1973) An American artist who specialized in modifying the natural landscape, often with the help of machinery. Most of his constructions were made from the same ground on which they were created.

TIEPOLO, Giovanni Battista (Giambattista) (1696-1770) Tiepolo's reputation rests on the wonderful frescoes, so full of light and colour, that adorn several royal palaces across Europe (including his native Venice). He is equally well known for his many altarpieces.

WYETH, N C (1882-1945) An American artist who produced more than 4000 illustrations, murals and paintings in his lifetime. He is particularly well known for his book illustrations of famous adventure stories.

Acknowledgements

With permission from the Rebecca Hossack Gallery, Fitzrovia, 17; Cordon Art BV, Baarn, Holland, 24; The Brotherton Collection, Leeds University Library, 25; Brandywine River Museum, 27; Ohio Historical Society, 29; Estate of Robert Smithson, courtesy of John Weber Gallery, New York/photo: Gianfranco Gorgoni, 33; Kettle's Yard, University of Cambridge, 36; David Armitage, 38; Fleetway Editions Ltd, 1996, 41; Image Select, 42; Cyan Inc., 43; © Universal City Studios Inc. Courtesy of MCA Publishing Rights, a Division of MCA Inc, 44. All other pictures are from the Bridgeman Art Library, courtesy of the following: National Gallery, London, 4; British Museum, London, 6; Private Collection/Giraudon/© DACS 1996, 7; Collection of R.R. Neuberger, New York/© Willem de Kooning/ARS, NY and DACS, London 1996, 8; Palazzo Sandi-Porto (Cipollato), Venice, 11; British Museum, London, 12; Werner Collection, Luton Hoo, Bedfordshire, 13; Palais de Tokyo, Paris, 14; Prado, Madrid, 18; Detroit Institute of Arts, Michigan, 19; Kunsthistorisches Museum, Vienna, 20; Edward James Foundation, Sussex/© Demart Pro Arte BV/DACS 1996, 21; National Gallery, London, 22; JCK Archive, London, 23; Private Collection, 28; National Gallery of Ireland, Dublin, 30; Private Collection, 32; Fitzwilliam Museum, University of Cambridge, 34; © 1996 ABC/Mondrian Estate/ Holtzman Trust. Licensed by ILP, 37; Staditsche Galerie im Lenbachhaus, Munich/© ADAGP, Paris and DACS, London 1996, 39.

Index